GROWING UP FAST

HOW NEW AGILE PRACTICES
CAN MOVE MARKETING AND INNOVATION
PAST THE OLD BUSINESS STALEMATES

BY JASCHA KAYKAS-WOLFF AND KEVIN FANN

ILLUSTRATION AND DESIGN BY SEAN MARTINEZ

CONTENTS

CHAPTER ONE
MARKETING AND INNOVATION

CHAPTER TWO
A QUICK AND DIRTY HISTORY OF BUSINESS MANAGEMENT

CHAPTER THREE
THE AGILE ERA: BEGINNING NOW?

CHAPTER FOUR
THE AGILE MINDSET

CHAPTER FIVE
THE AGILE TOOLBOX

CHAPTER SIX
DRUMMER NEEDED

Mom and Dad are fighting again.

That's what is happening in the world,
especially in the world of business.

Dad with his bottom-line schemes,
his stories with the boys down at the club,
his belief that nothing would happen
without his individual ego.

Mom with her rules and forecasting,
her compass for what should happen next,
her belief that nothing will happen
without a solid plan.

Dad's reminiscence of past victories,
shrouded with a credo that
past performance is no indication of
future performance.

Mom's obsession with an ideal future,
mixed with the faith that fairness and equality
can remain ever-fixed marks against
a sea of decay.

They both want control, and
they have control in different ways.

This book is about their brilliant overgrown kid
who takes apart toaster ovens and
still lives at home above the garage.
The kid who is both halves and neither of them,
whose life is passing by in waiting to act.
A wunderkind on ice.

"It's all risk and reward in the free market.
 Only the strong survive."
There you go again, Dad.

"Why don't you write down your goals. Things will work out.
 It takes a village."
There you go again, Mom.

Tinkering.
Exploring.
Frustrated.
Thoughtful.

Full of ephemeral ideas. Without solid roots.

For our families and colleagues. For ourselves.
It's time to move out of the house.

CHAPTER ONE

MARKETING AND INNOVATION

A World of Complementary Opposites

"Business has only two functions—marketing and innovation. Everything else is costs."

That quotation is either from business management consultant Peter Drucker or novelist Milan Kundera. It's attributed to both.

Kundera. Drucker.
Artistic novelist. Practical business consultant.
Marketing. Innovation.

The main irony about Mom and Dad—regulation and free-market, long-term planning and short-term gambles, the incessant worry about the future and the insistence of what worked in the past—is that they are a kind of complementary opposite to one another.

And the world exists because of complementary opposites.

- Light and dark.
- Energy and matter.
- Positive and negative.

These are the elements of the natural world, and without one there cannot be the other.

In business, the complementary process is to figure out how something works (innovation) and how to provide it to those who might find it useful (marketing). Marketing and innovation

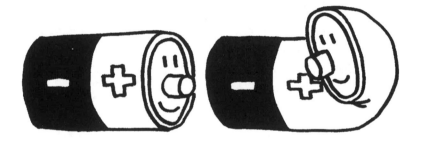

are intricately linked, and the interplay between the two is like the yin and yang of the business world. Marketing and innovation, when successful, create each other.

Consider UC Berkeley professor Terrence Deacon's description of replication in all living things and how it works.

> Although it is generally believed that polynucleotide chains like DNA and RNA molecules constitute life's replicators, they do not replicate themselves. To be more explicit: polynucleotide A cannot directly produce another exact duplicate of itself.

> Polynucleotide molecule A *can* produce a complementary polynucleotide molecule B, which in turn under the same conditions can produce polynucleotide molecule A.

This is the way marketing and innovation should interact.

Marketing cannot produce more and better marketing alone, just as engineering cannot produce more innovation alone. The two produce each other in a replicating system of complementary opposites.

If one tries to do it without the other, the system is too unstable. In studies of replicators where A makes itself—and makes a bad duplicate—the population has virtually no chance to survive.

When A makes B, however, and when B in turn makes A again, the stability of the system is exponentially more robust and able to change over time, because a mutation in B doesn't *necessarily* doom the system to failure.

YIN
AND YANG
OF THE
BUSINESS
WORLD

A small change in B doesn't destroy its ability to make A as certainly as when A makes itself.

These "failures" are what makes adaptation and life itself possible—the growth and change resulting from small mutations.

The interplay of two complementary forces—that's how marketing and innovation must work together.

> To try new things.
> To find what works and what doesn't.
> To change in small trials for better adaptations in the marketplace.
> To make life better through better business.

"Marketing is too important to be left to the marketing people."

So said David Packard of HP. What he meant was, engineers trying to invent new things cannot leave marketing those inventions to the marketing department, and yet they also can't invent new things properly without marketing's information.

New ideas shouldn't be invented in one department and then thrown over the wall to another department without the complementary interactions, because innovation is too important to be left to the engineering people, too.

If marketers shouldn't market innovations without the engineers involved, as Packard suggests, then engineers shouldn't innovate without marketers involved.

"FAILURES"
MAKE ADAPTATION
AND LIFE ITSELF
POSSIBLE

Engineering tends to make whatever it wants and tell marketing to go sell it. Marketing can't sell it and tries to tell engineering to change what it's making. They divide into two camps—meritocratic, political, hyper-rational, hyper-emotive. They use two different languages and internal squabbles begin.

Mom and Dad are fighting again.

"The aim of marketing is to make selling unnecessary." Drucker said. Sales costs are the cost of bad marketing and flawed innovation.

In proper combination, innovation creates marketing opportunities, which create innovation, which creates marketing opportunities, which create innovation, which creates marketing, and on and on.

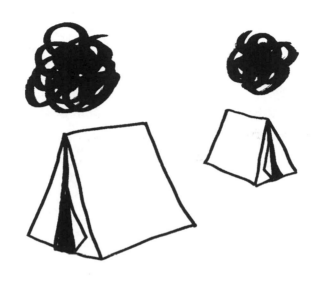

TWO CAMPS
SQUABBLING

What's This About Milkshakes?

A fast food chain was selling milkshakes. They could see the milkshakes were popular, but they suspected there was an opportunity to sell more of them. They could make their milkshakes thinner or thicker, bigger or smaller, with more chunks of delicious goodies in them or no chunks at all.

What should they do?

After studying their customers, market research told them they should do all those things. Make the milkshakes both bigger and smaller, both thinner and thicker, both loaded with chunks of fruit and chocolate and without any chunks at all.

How could that be?

Because there were two very different markets for the milkshakes:

1. Morning Commuters and
2. Nice-Guy Dads.

Morning Commuters needed something to sip during their daily drive that would start thick and get thin slowly, last long enough to keep them satisfied behind the wheel, and come with extra chunks of goodness to substitute for breakfast.

Nice-Guy Dads, on the other hand, were usually divorced men without custody who needed something they could buy their kids after a meal—a little extra "Dad's a nice guy" something—to make everyone feel better about the situation.

But Nice-Guy Dads were having to wait too long for the kids to slurp down thick milkshakes, and bigger sizes and slower melting and extra goodies sticking in the straw would only compound the wait. (These Nice-Guy Dads wanted to be nice, but not sit forever waiting for the kids to finish up!)

So the fast food chain made thicker, chunkier, bigger milkshakes for one market and smaller, thinner, smoother milkshakes for another. Bigger straws for the bigger chunks, and bigger straws for finishing up a small treat faster.

Magic! Revenues (and consumer waistbands) expanded.

If anyone at the fast food company had held too closely to the innovation of thickening the milkshake, they would have missed half the market.

If anyone had held too closely to selling the delicious chunks, they would have missed half the market.

This milkshake thinking is an example of the kind of thinking we need in the standoff between Mom and Dad. We need both solutions. And of course, we all need bigger straws.

Structural Minds vs. Exploratory Minds

There seem to be two basic types of mindsets in the workplace: structural and exploratory. Recent brain research shows we all have a practical and an emotional mind operating in tandem in our brains at the same time.

The structural mind is reliable and stable. Structure is the scaffolding and bones of a company, ensuring procedures are followed, schedules are met, paperwork is handled, and the bills are paid every quarter.

The exploratory mind, on the other hand, can't help but say, "What if?" to stability, seek out new approaches, and try novel solutions.

And the exploratory minds are usually wrong—almost always wrong (if there is such a thing) when making a first attempt at something new. But that's the greatest part of creativity's valor: learning from failure.

As big business and big government have outsourced exploration, they have also cut structure to the bone. Structure is great for the *status quo*, but it does nothing for the inquisitive urge to solve new problems.

Most of us were trained from early ages to think of high-success rates as most desirable. In school, 90% or better is an A.

PRACTICAL   EMOTIONAL

We're encouraged by big numbers and high rates of success, but sometimes safe numbers can lead you off the cliff.

Marketing and innovating for new opportunities is a series of adjustments to many small failures, where even a 5% success rate could be considered an A+, not 90% or better!

A branch will grow toward the light, but it must twist as it grows, finding the path of least constraint. Constraint almost always wins, and the branch can't grow everywhere at the same time.

Call it trial-and-error. Call it perseverance. Call it agile design. Call it entrepreneurship and wealth creation. Call it DNA replication. It's all the same: small learning against small failed attempts leading up to the explosion of a new opportunity and leafy greens.

The odds are low, but the upside is huge.

And the world needs constraints. We all need structure. But we also need the occasional bloom, where we can try and not be afraid to make mistakes, as long as the mistakes are new ones.

This is the mantra of agile business practice.

AS LONG AS
THE MISTAKES ARE
NEW ONES

In *Harvard Business Review*, Leonard Schlesinger listed six ways entrepreneurs can start small and stay agile as they try to find new ways to solve business problems.

1. Use the means at hand with the people and skills you already know.
2. Stay within an acceptable limit of loss, both real costs and opportunity costs.
3. Get the least amount of commitment you need to move forward.
4. Only bring in volunteers who share an interest in the new project—the make-it-happen people and help-it-happen people (leaving the let-it-happen people and keep-it-from-happening people out of it if they don't want to be involved.)
5. Link what you're doing to a business need and show results early.
6. Don't over-promise what the final results will be.

I discuss the history of business management and agile's emergence in software development in a later chapter, but it helps to introduce the term "agile" here. Schlesinger's six points show how this new approach to solving business problems requires us to relax our faith in deliberate strategies, in favor of adding an element of emergent strategy and exploration into the equation.

Professor Amar Bhide writes in *The Origin and Evolution of New Businesses* that 93% of all companies that ultimately became successful beyond a start-up phase had to abandon their original strategy.

93% of successful start-up businesses abandoned their original plan in order to become successful.

Why? Because 93% of the time the original plan was wrong. The deliberate strategy eventually gave way to a better, emergent strategy.

In the agile world, success doesn't mean knowing exactly what the plan is before you begin. Success instead means having enough money left over to try an emergent opportunity after the deliberate plan has failed.

This requires business management to allow for exploratory processes to coexist in the same mind as structural processes— a dual operating system, where both work in complementary opposite fashion.

The goal? To get done what needs to get done today, and still have enough flexibility (and money) to go after the emerging idea tomorrow.

IKEA Gets the Job Done

IKEA is not a furniture store. They do sell furniture, that's true, but what IKEA really sells is the ability to furnish an entire room in one afternoon.

With entire warehouses set up as staged worlds customers can step into, IKEA realized they *could* sell sofas and chairs and kitchen utensils, or they could do the hard part for their customers, which was to put all of these things together in a world people could experience.

IKEA customers can put themselves in a whole new world without having to use their imagination to put the many different pieces of that world together.

Countless furniture stores have come and gone trying to sell furniture. IKEA has thrived on seeing the problem in a different light, allowing the deliberate strategy of selling furniture to evolve into an emergent strategy of selling furnished rooms.

I don't know how long it took this strategy to emerge, but the company does it so well, their customers have become evangelists—to the benefit of dorm rooms and guest bedrooms across the world.

That brand loyalty comes more from IKEA doing the job customers need them to do, not from IKEA products alone.

3M and the Lead User Process

Minnesota Mining and Manufacturing has a reputation for decades of innovative success, from Scotch tape in the 1920s to Post-it Notes and Thinsulate in the 1970s. Many of these products came from the exploratory minds in the engineering lab.

But in the 1990s, 3M asked, "Why can't product developers come up with breakthroughs more regularly?" The structural minds were trying to find a rhyme and reason to the exploratory process. In doing so, they recognized two things:

1. Companies have a strong incentive to focus on the short-term, incremental improvements of existing products.
2. Innovators have no set system for coming up with new ideas.

But 3M didn't want to focus only on improving existing products. They set a goal of having 30% of company annual sales come from products that didn't exist four years before. The innovators at 3M needed marketing to help them figure out where these new ideas could come from, and the answer was in what the company called "lead users."

Lead users are the tinkerers of the world. Lead users come up with functioning prototypes of the gadgets they need rather than wait for a company to make the gadget for them.

3M identified lead users by networking across different areas of industry, to find out who was doing interesting things with their products. They began to think of lead users as third-party R & D that the company could select based on company needs.

3M marketers began to collect information, not from the center of any one market, but from the outliers of markets. They networked in what the company calls their "pyramid of expertise," going from lead user to lead user in many different industries: from medical imaging to semiconductor imaging, pattern-recognition research to the military.

By definition, these lead users are on the fringes—albeit creative, innovative fringes—and finding a true lead user is rare. So 3M reached out. They listened. They followed. They held workshops to get to know lead users better, wherever they turned up.

Employing this lead user process, 3M developed many new products that were already being used in prototype form, helping them bring to market new innovations such as surgical drapes, thin adhesive-backed plastic films that adhere to skin at the site of surgical incisions and isolate the area from infection.

A kind of surgical Scotch tape was already being used and had a market before 3M "invented" it.

How Google and Apple Kiss

Google requires its engineers to spend 20% of every week on a project outside their normal work. Something they are interested in. Something passionate. Something unknown.

The only stipulation? "Don't be evil." End of story.

History will determine whether Google's employees can meet that criterium or not. Meanwhile, the company continues to create and run a solid, innovative business.

But the most striking thing about Google's caveat, besides how they may ultimately fail to uphold it, is how utterly simple it is. One rule: Don't be evil. In a world of complementary opposites, it's remarkable that some of the most successful people to deal in complex technology have simplicity at their core.

In his book, *Insanely Simple: The Obsession That Drives Apple's Success*, creative director Ken Segall recounts many instances in which Steve Jobs settled complicated matters at Apple by "hitting it with the Simple Stick."

- Why make a phone with three buttons, instead of one?
- Why argue the five points in a commercial, when there should be only one?
- Why call it the "DVP SR200P/B," instead of "iPhone"?

According to Segall, Jobs was obsessive about simplicity, making things easy to understand, purchase, and use. And who can argue with his results? Through simplicity, Jobs led a company that changed how we interact with the complexities that surround, connect, and engulf us. And he put it in our pocket.

Segall compares the battle in terms of good and evil. "Unlike Simplicity, which usually presents itself with a certain elegance, Complexity can get ugly. Even worse, it can never die. But the good news is, neither can Simplicity. It's capable of defeating any challenge from the dark side—it just needs someone to fight on its behalf."

Don't be fooled. Simplicity, like agile business itself, is *more difficult* than the alternative. It's harder to do and harder to maintain "simple," because it's easy to acquiesce to the dark force of Complexity when it comes calling.

As Jobs himself said, "You have to work hard to get your thinking clean to make it simple. But it's worth it in the end, because once you get there, you can move mountains."

Let's do that.

The Dual Operating System

Agile is a systematic way to meet the practical, day-to-day needs of a business, while still preserving some impractical time to explore new opportunities and experiment with new ideas.

But let's be honest: Whether due to real or imagined constraints, most businesses "don't have the time or the money" to experiment. Not everyone is a 3M or a Google. It's better that they aren't.

But without experimentation, *status quo* businesses eventually lose to disruptive businesses. Not experimenting based on new ideas is like saying you're too busy at work to grow and change in your personal life.

This creates what author Walter Kiechel III says is the major innovation challenge looming over 21st-century business:

How do you find ways to free the spark of creativity from the tidal pull to do the same old thing?

This is especially challenging for businesses that have outsourced innovative thinkers and retained those who follow the company line, which has on one hand created stability and authority, but on the other created a homogenous, inertial mass with few new ideas.

Most companies beyond the startup phase get optimized for efficiencies, not the ability to capitalize on opportunities and dodge new market threats. For mature companies, failure almost always comes in the same form: The organization faces a threat

TIDAL PULL

or opportunity, and they try to cram for a transformation using some process that worked in the past.

That is to say, for most companies, Mom and Dad start fighting again about who messed up.

Traditional management processes work well for day-to-day operations like planning, budgeting, defining jobs, hiring and firing, shuttling the paperwork, and measuring and reporting results.

What traditional management is very poor at doing is identifying threats and opportunities early enough to create and act on strategic initiatives. They tend to cling to habits, fear loss of power and stature, crave stability and default to what they know best: the hierarchy.

The solution to hierarchical stalemate is not more hierarchy, but for companies to develop a complementary agile management practice alongside the hierarchy—two systems operating in concert:

The Structural System: run by the traditional hierarchy, managing daily demands, doing the things that are necessary to keep the lights on and keep Mom and Dad nice and comfortable.

The Exploratory System: run as a connection of networks, agile in its experimentation, continually questioning the business, the industry, and the organization, to keep the next generation challenged and engaged.

CRAM FOR A TRANSFORMATION

CLING TO THE HIERARCHY

These two systems operate in the same house. They don't oppose each other. They aren't "either/or," but "both/and." They are the complementary opposites of the agile era of business.

In his book *Thinking Fast and Slow*, Nobel-laureate Daniel Kahneman presents evidence that shows our brains work in a similar way—as two coordinated systems—one rational, one emotional. And recognizing threats and opportunities is as much an emotional matter as a rational one.

In the book *Switch*, Chip and Dan Heath talk about a dysfunctional dual-operating system using the Elephant and Rider metaphor, where the Rider is the rational mind, deciding where he wants to go and presenting a logical, reasonable plan for how to get there.

But the Elephant? The Elephant is emotional.

The Elephant doesn't respond to well-reasoned arguments. The Elephant wants an emotional reason to charge, but the rational Rider can't seem to give him one. The Rider treats the Elephant like a machine.

What happens?

The Rider gets frustrated, and the Elephant doesn't move. And when you've got both Mom and Dad trying to move the Elephant, they start fighting about who's doing a worse job at it.

When important opportunities and threats eventually pop up, the Riders are powerless to motivate action. Isn't this the nature of the stalemate we see in most businesses today?

TOO BUSY
TO GROW

8 Steps For Establishing A Dual-Operating System

In *Harvard Business Review's* "The Big Idea: Accelerate," John P. Kotter lists eight necessary elements required for traditional businesses to develop an exploratory culture within their hierarchical structures.

Though I have adapted them slightly, I believe these eight steps also apply to establishing an agile network within hierarchical structures, because agile is exploratory by nature.

Step 1. Create a sense of urgency.

The business opportunity or threat must be urgent enough to prompt action. Think of the Elephant. He runs on emotions. Find a threat or opportunity he can get into. This first step is critical.

Step 2. Establish a guiding coalition.

For those who want to be part of the new agile network, they must come from various departments and have broad levels of responsibility and authority within the hierarchy. And, most importantly, members of the coalition should be volunteers to the agile network. This is a "want-to" group of people, not a "have-to" group.

Step 3. Have a vision through the development of initiatives, questions to ask, and tests to try.

Whatever the business opportunity, develop an idea of what you expect your explorations might turn up. Even if they are wrong, they should serve a natural urge to know. The vision should pique interests and curiosities.

Step 4. Communicate the vision for buy-in from the rest of the agile group and the company as a whole.

State your hypotheses clearly. They don't have to be spot-on, but they do have to be interesting. Give everyone an idea of why you chose some initiative to explore, and then choose a good writer in the group who can express the idea in plain language.

Step 5. Empower broad-based action.

The power of the hierarchy is also its biggest weakness. All the decision making is relegated to the top. In the agile network, ideas and expertise can come from anyone. Although there is a guiding coalition, the object is to remove barriers, not maintain a chain-of-command. That impulse to chains is the hierarchy trying to regain control.

Step 6. Celebrate small, visible, short-term wins.

Your agile network won't last long unless you show value fairly quickly. Skeptics will be quick to crush your efforts, so don't go big right away. Do something small. Pick an attainable initiative. Do it well. Practice the agile process. Build momentum.

Step 7. Don't let up.

You might need a victory, but don't declare too much of a victory too soon. Agile is about learning from mistakes and readjusting. Keep pushing forward, because when you take your foot off the gas, that's when cultural and political resistance will arise. Make time for your network initiatives. Stick to it, no matter how much routine busy-work pops up.

THE URGE
TO KNOW

THE IMPULSE
TO CHAINS

Step 8. Incorporate the changes and the lessons learned into the culture of the business as a whole.

This is how the agile network can really inform an entrenched hierarchy. When you find better ways to do something or new opportunities to pursue, work them into the other side of the dual-operating system.

When implementing these eight steps, Kotter says there are three guiding principles to keep in mind.

Remember: The eight steps are non-sequential.

These steps are a model, not a process or procedure—a shape, not an orderly progression. All eight steps should happen, but they don't have to happen in any particular order. Don't lose steam worrying too much about order.

Remember: The agile network must be made up of a volunteer army.

About 10% of the workforce will suffice, as long as the people in the agile network want to be there. Don't be exclusive or closed to participation, but also don't repeatedly try to recruit people who are structurally minded, because they won't enjoy being in an agile work group, and they won't see the value of it.

Kotter says, "The volunteer army is not a bunch of grunts carrying out orders from the brass. Its members are change leaders who bring energy, commitment, and enthusiasm." By "brass," he means Mom and Dad.

THE
BRASS

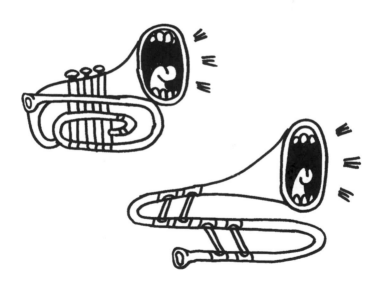

Remember: The agile operating system is made up of workers who work within the hierarchy, too.

The agile network has a guiding coalition at the center and initiatives and sub-initiatives that orbit around it, coming together and disbanding as needed. The agile network cannot be viewed as a "rogue operation," or the hierarchy will inevitably crush it.

Establishing a dual-operating system attunes businesses for better vision, opportunity, response, inquiry, curiosity, inspired action and celebration.

It DOES NOT double the project management, budget reviews, reporting, chains of command, compensation or accountability. It DOES create two systems within one organization that complement, rather than duplicate, each other.

Ideally, workers who thrive in the agile network can bring that newfound energy to the hierarchy, too.

The new agile network may at first feel like one big, soft, squishy, employee-engagement exercise. That's fine! It evolves. It's not a sudden or dramatic change. Like team-building exercises, it takes a certain level of comfort and trust developed over time.

Keep going. Keep the steps small. Communicate the victories from the start. Get your feet underneath you while you sell the agile network to the existing hierarchy. If you do all this, the business value will emerge before the hierarchy can dismiss it as silly, different, a waste of time, whatever.

Besides, today's "waste of time" can quickly uncover tomorrow's great idea.

CHAPTER TWO

A QUICK AND DIRTY HISTORY OF BUSINESS MANAGEMENT

Agile means, "Try anything, but never fail the same way twice."

Systematic innovation is at the core of all agile practices, even though the term is somewhat an oxymoron. Sparks of innovation don't easily coexist with systematic approaches; systematic approaches don't necessarily produce sparks of innovation.

The goal of systematic innovation builds on a long history of systematic changes in business management, spanning several different eras that began and which have evolved in the U.S. over the past 100 years or so.

The Efficiency Era: Business management begins as a quasi-engineering efficiency study in the wake of late 19th-century monopolies and robber-baron largesse.

The Social Era: A time of great prosperity and hope, where businesses served as a collective mechanism for social reforms and widespread increases in living standards after World War II.

The Shareholder Value Era: Beginning with the deregulation in the 1980s, American business went through a period of sacrosanct ideology about shareholder value, "greed is good," and the rise of great income disparities between management and workers.

I would add a new era to that list:

The Agile Era: A combination of all those past management eras, now dominated by a rising need for systematic innovation using the most responsive business practices.

Agile has a new management ethic. Agile promotes networks over hierarchies, creativity over uniformity, human over mechanism, and customer need over political agenda.

How did we get here?

Historians generally point to one event as the symbolic birth of business management: The meeting of the American Society of Mechanical Engineers, Chicago, May 1886, where Henry R. Towne, cofounder of the Yale Lock Manufacturing Company, proposed the idea of codifying a "management of works" as a way to apply engineering principles to business production.

Towne's presentation was significant because he formalized two main points of business management:

1. Management consists of a set of practices that can be studied and improved.
2. Management should be rooted in classical economics and the efficient use of resources.

Towne's audience was almost exclusively engineers—a rational, literal, logical bunch.

The Efficiency Era: 1880s—1940

The first decades of business management were dominated by dreams of scientific exactitude. Notable companies from this period were American Sugar, American Telephone and Telegraph Company, General Electric, Allied Chemical, International Harvester, U.S. Steel, Union Carbide, Sears Roebuck, Western Union.

The efficiency era came on the heels of the "robber-baron" period in American capitalism, a climate dominated by monopoly, corruption, and exorbitant wealth from men whose last names are infamous: Carnegie, Vanderbilt, Rockefeller, Morgan, Mellon, Stanford, Astor.

A rising middle class in the U.S. began to push against these political bosses and robber barons, with progressives ideas about bringing the wisdom of science and process to business.

In 1911, Frederick Taylor wrote *Principles of Scientific Management*, in which he advocated applying the scientific method to business.

Taylor first outlined the difference between "numbers people" and "people people" and pointed to that divide as the key tension in the workplace. He also asserted that those differences between the quantifiable and the human shouldn't be adversaries, but rather, complementary opposites.

There was a general belief that all businesses could be operated in the "one best way" if scientific processes were followed, but studies uncovered the mysteries of human psychology at work, as well.

This early Efficiency Era was marked by overt classism, where those in management believed their rise to power was the answer to The Great Depression, inept government, and the changes being brought on in the world by global social upheaval.

Sound familiar?

Dim the Lights and Show You Care

An early Efficiency Era study on worker productivity showed that turning the lights in a factory up or down increased worker productivity.

Lights up or lights down—it didn't matter which, because it wasn't the lighting level that increased productivity. It was the perception by the factory workers that management was paying attention to them.

Any attention from management was good for productivity.

Later studies showed productivity would also increase the most when:

1. Workers coalesced into a group.
2. Management solicited feedback and suggestions.

The Social Era: 1940—1980

The era of business management following World War II and ending with the Reagan presidency was marked by overall confidence, public support, and good feelings about the potential for business to improve life, with employment linked to social stability, health care, housing, and the social contract with labor unions.

Notable companies during this period were General Foods, Eastman Kodak, Proctor & Gamble, United Aircraft, Chrysler, Woolworth, and Goodyear.

The Social Era also saw the rise of some important business management scholars, especially Peter Drucker.

Many consider Peter Drucker the father of modern management, with several important publications during his life, including:

Concept of the Corporation (1946)
The Practice of Management (1954)
Managing for Results (1964)

Concept of the Corporation was the first book to delve into large corporations and how they impact society on a broad level. *Managing for Results* may have been the first book on business strategy.

Drucker said, "Business exists to produce results," and the work of management should be to always look for opportunities.

Drucker also saw the corporation as a social network, and believed business had two functions: innovation and marketing, ideas that remain critical to agile business practices in our own time.

His strategies were a throwback to Taylorism and strict measurement—not just of worker productivity—but of everything. And it worked! By the end of the 1970s, the 200 largest firms in the U.S. accounted for over 60% of total business sales, employment, and income.

Also influential during this time of great promise for American business was Mary Parker Follett, a social worker, management consultant, and pioneer in the fields of organizational theory and organizational behavior.

Her ideas of "constructive confrontation" or "win-win" situations remain with us, though Follett coined the term "win-win" as a mechanism for integrating solutions, not a synonym for political compromise. Follett also loathed micromanagement, calling it "bossism."

Douglas McGregor was another scholar who saw the action of opposites in the workplace, developing his "Theory X/Theory Y" as representations of philosophical extremes of pure control and pure autonomy.

Theory X said, "People are lazy and need policing" in the workplace. Theory Y countered, "People seek meaning in work and contribute based on positive design."

These two extremes still struggle against one another.

The Shareholder Value Era: 1980—current

In the 1980s, business retreated from broad social involvement in favor of market specialization and servitude to market forces. Business declined in moral ambitions, with a decline in union power, globalization, the rise of MBA degrees, and an overall obsession with shareholder value.

The Shareholder Value Era ushered in deregulation in transportation—airlines, railroads, and trucking—as well as deregulation in telecommunications and finance. The importation of cars, steel, and consumer electronics rose sharply, followed by an unprecedented age of technology and the rise of personal computer hardware and software.

Junk bonds and financial takeovers became standard practice without constraints, percolating through a "greed is good" societal undertone. Management began to change, with heavier and heavier emphasis on shareholders, often to the detriment of stakeholder interests.

Corporate management's clearest goal since the 1980s has been to create wealth for shareholders and reward managers who played by those rules with ownership incentives and stock options.

By 1999, stock options accounted for 50% of executive pay. The ratio of CEO pay to average worker pay went through the roof in the U.S., peaking at over 500:1 in 2000 according to research from the Institute for Policy Studies.

In 1985, the term "value creation" first arose in business strategy circles to justify exorbitant corporate paychecks. CEOs, the logic went, created the value and therefore should enjoy the spoils of the business profit—as measured by the increase in company stock price.

This period also saw the rise of information technology, growing from small data management firms to the all-pervasive sea of data that runs through every department of modern business today.

More than just networks and servers, IT connected businesses directly to billions of customers in an easily measured and trackable way, an ability that has only increased with more social media outlets and mobile technology.

CHAPTER THREE

THE AGILE ERA: BEGINNING NOW?

As we come to the end of the Shareholder Value Era, business focus has shifted from the somewhat robotic efficiency measures and philosophical high-mindedness of previous eras to one that now values two things above all else: leadership and innovation.

Innovation is the 21st century gold standard. And it probably should be. Leadership, on the other hand, is a much grayer area.

Hardline proponents of shareholder value still cling to stock price. It guides their decisions, tells them exactly how they are doing, and comforts them on cold evenings. It's directly measurable.

But human behaviorists and "leaders"—and count the agile among them—seem to be all over the map. If trying to run a "customer-focused" business proves to be a fad, it will join many others that have appeared on mainstream bookstore shelves over the past 20 years, with themes like:

"navigating change"
"the wisdom of teams and power of loyalty"
"running a learning organization"
"core competencies"
"delighting customers"
"moving the cheese"

And maybe "agile" will eventually fall upon the cliche pyre, too. But agile's a little different. By design, agile business management tries to maintain a safe haven for that spark of innovation to happen, allowing flashes of human insight beyond analytical calculation, though somehow driven by analytical calculation. Agile is more a process than a catch phrase.

Agile business management strives to make the innovator's spark possible by taking small steps and testing a broad range of opportunities—small risks that change often, rather than a giant hierarchical strategy imposed from above.

As a society, we are objectively better off due to the 100-year rise of business management in terms of literacy gains, poverty rates, food production, and average quality of life.

However, as Walter Kiechel III writes in "The Management Century," there are big challenges ahead in the U.S. and in the world—challenges that *status quo* shareholder-value measures may not be able to address.

> How are we going to create jobs for everyone who wants one?
> How are we going to adjust to environmental change?
> How will we deal with the new normal, which is constant change?
> Can we maximize returns in a world where there is no "one best way"?
> Why should we trust business to try to solve these problems?
> And what is business management's source of authority?

Hierarchy, wealth, and notions of innate intellectual superiority fell short in previous eras because, as Kiechel says, business lacked a "moral resonance" earlier generations of workers had hoped for.

Can agile achieve a kind of resonance? Time will tell.

What Exactly is Agile?

The roots of Agile grew at the beginning of the Shareholder Value Era, when high-tech Western companies adopted Eastern management practices, beginning in the late-1980s.

Influenced by the success of Japanese consumer electronics and auto makers, firms in the U.S. started switching from high-inventory, huge-capacity, low-customization models of business to more "lean" manufacturing.

Lean manufacturing—or "kanban" or "just-in-time" or "six sigma"—emphasized making products according to immediate demand, responding to the pull of the market rather than trying to push products onto the market after they had already been manufactured.

Lean manufacturing also meant reducing inventories, the amount of raw materials firms had sitting around waiting to make products with.

Why was inventory reduction so key? Because if the market changes and suddenly nobody wants white vinyl boots anymore, then you're stuck holding the bag if you have a warehouse full of white vinyl.

Reducing inventory was also the easiest way for businesses to improve their RONA, or Return on Net Assets, a measure equal to a firm's income divided by its assets.

Return on Net Assets = Income/Assets

If increasing RONA was a sacred goal of the Shareholder Value Era, there's an easy way and a hard way to achieve that. One way is to increase sales. That's hard. Requires innovation and marketing.

But if you lower the amount of assets you have—or "go lean"—that's a much easier way to increase RONA, and it's not as psychological as sales. It's practical. Thus, businesses began to outsource assets, both inventory and capital equipment, as well as personnel and payroll.

Denominators in the equation went down, and RONA measures went up. The results were mixed, and we're still seeing the ramifications—where some industries *needed* to go lean, other industries have gone so lean they've nearly put themselves out of business.

Then came the software boom.

Agile development became the best way to make software. With all the versioning, continuous improvements, and going to market with minimum viability, software was a natural industry for agile process development and for agile management practices.

Scrums, sprints, data visualizations, exploratory teams—all of these things seem intuitive to software developers, because it's the process required to do the work properly. Agile business can change course when a new opportunity arises, and nowhere have new opportunities come and gone as fast as in software development.

Software attracts people with gifted analytical minds, but they also tend to stew in contemplation over the contingencies of how to start a new project. Sometimes this is called "procrastination," but that's not fair. It's more a cycle of deliberation and analysis paralysis. (And no mind works harder to find reasons why something "won't work" than the hyper-analytical mind!)

To get around that tendency to analyze too much, agile processes break big analytical matters into small steps with emphasis on:

- Short review cycles
- Many iterations to improve and change
- Willingness to try something new with the understanding that nothing is final (or doesn't have to be)
- Optimism to go with the best idea at the time
- Discipline to do the next right thing and not look back at mistakes as wastes of time.

Agile Era businesses have to get something out there in the world and test it—usually with digital channels because they are large, measurable, responsive, and inexpensive—and then move on based on what they've learned.

Virginia Mason Medical Center and Going Lean Gone Right

The healthcare execs at Virginia Mason Medical took a field trip to Japan, and when they came back and implemented certain changes they had learned there, metrics at their healthcare facilities improved. Things once left unmeasured became measurable gains.

Inspired by seeing the Toyota Production System first-hand, leaders at Virginia Mason Medical Center in Seattle instituted performance monitoring, measurement, and weekly team meetings.

These simple steps dramatically improved patient care at the hospital. For example, in the breast clinic the lead times—from initial patient call to final diagnosis—fell from three weeks to three days.

Not coincidentally, the hospital soon returned to profitability after years and years of successive losses after going lean.

But why wouldn't all hospitals go lean?
Isn't that the kind of reform we need in health care?

It is. But as Harvard Business School professor Clayton Christiansen points out in his book *How Will You Measure Your Life?* the medical industry lacks a prime motivator for reforms like "lean" manufacturing: competition.

Most regional areas are served by one hospital and one hospital only. That takes hospitals out of a competitive market, like that of technology or software, and puts them more in the world of monopoly business practices.

If you don't have to go lean, you won't, especially if you don't take it on as a matter of principle the way the management at Virginia Mason did—you probably won't.

Hospitals are behind that curve, and we have a big problem in this country with healthcare in part because of that.

But there is some hope. Doctors have begun to use technology like texting and electronic medical records to provide patient care similar to times when family doctors made house calls and really knew patients on a personal level.

For hospitals to go lean doesn't mean they treat their patients like Toyotas on an assembly line. Quite the opposite. Going lean allows more personal care and value to reach the patients on both a physical and psychological level.

Main Street, Mad Men, and Marketing History

Going lean (and doing things like using technology and communication innovations to provide better service) seems obvious to digital marketers and software developers who are at the forefront of technology.

But other industries aren't the same. They don't emphasize exploratory problem-solving as much as structural control. In industries like healthcare, the management model seems to be stuck in inefficient processes, standardized procedures, and heavy bureaucracy.

They have what I call the Mad Men idea of management: one big idea for successful strategy, devised by a few people who are smarter than others and handed down to be implemented as though chiseled in stone.

The television show "Mad Men" has a character who represents the mythical big-idea man in Don Draper. Draper is an uber-creative genius at an ad firm on Madison Avenue in the 1960s. Mad Men is popular for many reasons: excellent writing, trendy styling, and insightful themes about the male-dominated—*white* male-dominated—society at the dawn of big changes in civil rights and gender equality in America.

The show is also popular because it represents a swan song to the big-idea mythology in business. When Don Draper wakes up with a bottle in one hand and a flash of insight—the a-ha moment!—for, say, Pan Am Airlines, he's fulfilling a role that will survive only in our fiction.

Another Fiction: Miller's General Store, At The Corner of Main and Maple

Before Don Draper, everybody loved Mr. Miller, the man who ran the general store in a time long past. With his clean shirt tucked behind his green canvas apron, Mr. Miller sold everything from avocado seeds to zip ties. We knew him when we were kids, and, though he'd lost a step over the years, by golly, old man Miller still kept a pen and scrap of paper at the ready to jot down and promise to get anything our hearts desired.

Consumers had a one-to-one relationship with Mr. Miller. He was part of the community. The next time you came in (slingshot in your back pocket, no doubt) Mr. Miller would reach behind the counter and present, like magic, the thing you had requested the visit before.

And he had it on hand the next time, too.

"Probably due for a fresh batch of hairpins, turpentine and gauze pads?" he'd say. He knew us so well. He spent a lot of time and money per person marketing on this small scale.

Then, radio and television made it possible to speak to a mass audience, ushering in an age of advertising and marketing represented by the Mad Men of the 1950s and 1960s. It suddenly became feasible to broadcast a commercial jingle to a massive "target" audience—namely, the people who could afford radios and televisions.

Businesses no longer had to understand individual customers. They could look at the world in terms of groups. "Don't be the only house on your block without a Whirlpool refrigerator."

With these mass targets came measures of how "close" marketing had come to hitting the mark: CPMs, share of viewership, demographics. The goal was to get the right message to the right people at the right time, as efficiently as possible.

The 1970s brought more innovations for collecting and crunching market data, using huge computer databases to measure and refine targeting. This was the dawn of direct marketing. Measure it. Test it. Tweak it. Print report on dot-matrix printer.

To the detriment of the Mad Men-style of selling the sizzle, these new direct marketing techniques could empirically trace direct sales, which was great, if all you were measuring were short-term sales of grilled-cheese grills and ab rockers.

But what about longer purchasing cycles?
Repeat customers?
Long-term effects for the brand?

Direct marketing had no answer for these kinds of questions.

Relationship marketing did, offering a profound shift in thinking: Customers don't buy products; they buy *into* products. They buy *into* brands. They buy an idea about themselves, and they are willing to pay a premium to have it reflected back upon them.

Relationship marketing forced marketers to think beyond market share to create brands consumers wanted as part of their lives. Businesses flocked to implement member programs, clubs, frequent visitor cards, secret sales, reward gifts, and punchcards.

By the 2000s, marketers had the technology to learn more information about consumers than just age, education level, and geographic area. Marketers now know what people like, what they look at online, what they order, what they return, what they send as a gift, what they Tweet, post, link to—an unbelievable amount of detail.

Mr. Miller never knew us this well! It's eerily personal.

But beyond digital data about customers, today's marketers also have to consider CRM data, retail sales data, overall economic data, employee performance data, stock performance data, the data that tells you how well you're collecting data, and metadata about how much of that data is worthwhile data.

With so much data, marketers have three choices:

1. Ignore it and perish
2. Consider only some of it and get lucky
3. Embrace it all and thrive.

Embracing all data and the agile process doesn't mean you have to know it all. Having the big idea isn't over, but marketers no longer have to pull it out of a storekeeper's apron or a dapper felt hat. Out of millions of small ideas, big ideas emerge.

PULL IT OUT OF
A DAPPER HAT

In fact, agile marketing means you have to know less. You don't have to be Don Draper Genius. Agile marketing comes from what businesses have learned by building software over the last 20 years: Give the world something that works as fast as possible, and be able to modify, evolve, improve and grow—ultimately striving to delight customers in a one-to-one way similar to Mr. Miller at his general store.

The Agile Era requires being able to use all our analytical information to take intuitive risks—to try things Mr. Miller and Don Draper never had the freedom or ability to try.

Big things, brave things.

Does Management Work?

Mom and Dad are fighting again. When it happens, a fair question pops up. Do we need management at all? Does management generally work?

No. Not if management only means power suits and celebrity leadership acting out an epic battle to accumulate cash into one big pile.

After all, the rest of us want to make something! We want to *do* something.

A recent study by Nicholas Bloom of Stanford University suggests that, if you've ever wondered what management actually does, you have good reason.

Bloom's research group, including Raffaella Sadun of Harvard Business School and John Van Reenen of the London School of Economics, tested whether thousands of businesses followed practices considered to be essential to good management.

After 10 years of studies from 100 researchers in 20 different countries covering 8000 medium-sized manufacturing firms with between 50 and 5000 employees, the results were unequivocal:

In Bloom's own words: "Poor management is rampant."

That's probably not a surprise to anyone, except maybe to the managers themselves.

POWER SUITS
AND
CELEBRITY
LEADERSHIP

The 3 Essential Elements of Good Management

Bloom ranked 8000 companies in his study on a scale, where each point from 1 to 5 represented a 23% rise in productivity, a 14% increase in market capitalization, and a 1.4% growth in annual sales. Scores of 5 were rare; 1's were plentiful.

Bloom found three best practices in the study data that correlated to good management:

1. **Targets**
   Does the organization in question support long-term goals with tough—but achievable—short-term benchmarks?
2. **Incentives**
   Does the organization reward high performers?
   Do they retrain or move under-performers?
3. **Monitoring**
   Does the organization collect performance data to identify opportunities for improvement?

A staggering majority of businesses don't know how to develop targets, create incentives to reach those targets, or monitor and measure progress.

"A call for 'better management' may not seem like a cutting-edge idea," Bloom says, "but given the potentially large effects on incomes, productivity and delivery of critically needed services worldwide, it may actually be a radical one."

As business managers, Mom and Dad either don't know they have a problem, or they can't be objective in evaluating their own skill level at taking on and solving problems.

For example, 79% of the 8000 organizations in Bloom's study claimed to have "above average" management practices. That's 79% of overwhelmingly poor business managers giving themselves the thumbs up. And Bloom also found no correlation between their self-assessment and their actual management scores. No correlation.

Not only does this expose Mom and Dad's rosy opinion of themselves, it also suggests the human tendency to believe like the children of Lake Woebegone: We're all above average.

Bloom's research shows management can improve and produce big financial gains from what's currently going to waste. In fact, improvements come fairly easy. When companies in the study received five months of heavy business consulting versus only one month of light consulting, the heavy consulting produced dramatically better business results.

But here's the rub: Many of the companies Bloom studied worked in textile and steel mill environments in global locations, where simple improvements like "inventory control" and "equipment maintenance"—having some, instead of none—produced vast improvements over the control group.

Agile environments more likely work in technology and software. What good could specific initiatives like those do for us?

A good boss—one who targets, offers incentives, and monitors progress—adds about 10% to worker productivity. That number comes from a study reported by Stephen Dubner on Freakonomics Radio. It doesn't mean much as an absolute number, but it does mean management makes a difference. Good management—as studies and experience will tell you—is rare, but when it works, it does work.

That 10% is the boss's contribution alone and applies to bosses who have direct contact with employees.

Figurehead leaders—like celebrity CEOs, presidents, and other Big Wigs—don't matter as much to worker productivity. And bad ones don't matter at all.

Do You Follow The Three Essential Elements of Good Management?

These questions were adapted from interviews in the study of over 8000 manufacturers in 20 countries. For more questions from the study, see *www.worldmanagementsurvey.org*

1. **Targeting**

    How do you communicate organizational goals to individual workers?

    Does anyone complain that the target definitions are too complex?

    How do you deal with repeated failures in a specific business segment?

2. **Incentives**

    How do senior managers show that attracting, developing, and retaining talent is a top priority?

    How long is underperformance tolerated?

    What makes it distinctive or special to work at your company?

    What does your company do about star performers who want to leave?

3. **Monitoring**

    How do problems get exposed and fixed?

    What key indicators do you use for performance tracking?

    For a given problem, how do you identify the root cause?

CHAPTER FOUR

THE AGILE MINDSET

Before talking about the component aspects of agile marketing and innovation—storytelling, hypothesis testing, customer purchase cycles, feedback, and backlogs—it's important first to mention the overall mindset needed for agile processes to thrive, including:

- The theory of capabilities
- Downward mobility
- Emergent strategies
- The difference between good money and bad money
- The difference between motivation and incentive
- The difference between full-value thinking and marginal thinking

The Theory of Capabilities

Harvard Business School professor Clayton Christiansen goes into great detail about The Theory of Capabilities in his book *How Will You Measure Your Life?* Christiansen says capabilities are composed of three things: Resources + Processes + Priorities

Resources—what you have to work with, including technology, skills, money, patents, people

Processes—how you work, such as hierarchies, lean networks, the dual operating system

Priorities—why you work, including company culture and values

In some ways, American business has been so awash in excess resources that our processes and priorities have suffered. We tend to think of solving a problem by throwing more money at it.

This is how both Mom and Dad operate—big budgets, big plans and big investments. But being agile means starting small and trying things that could rarely survive a big-ticket vetting, budgeting and approval processes.

Agile is a process, and as such, an attempt to bring our work into balance by redirecting resources and priorities to solve problems. One big part of that, Clayton says, is to focus on what your business suppliers are trying to do in the future, rather than what they're doing today, so that you can keep your in-house capabilities strong—especially your processes.

Dell and Going Lean Gone Wrong

Outsourcing helped Dell increase company revenue while decreasing assets, making the company a wildly profitable computer manufacturer in the late 1990s to mid-2000s.

But Dell management outsourced and outsourced until the company owned virtually nothing but a brand. They outsourced valuable company capabilities, especially the process of learning how to solve problems, which their vendors learned while serving Dell itself.

The story of Dell Computer—and the American semiconductor industry, as a whole—is an example of going lean the wrong way.

While working with Taiwanese electronics firm Asus, Dell began by outsourcing the more routine tasks of computer manufacturing—component-level stuff—to increase the company's RONA metric and stock price.

But Asus wasn't a passive lackey. Asus may have started off by doing simple things for Dell, but they gradually moved from down-market supplier to up-market innovator, undercutting the bigger, more lethargic Dell.

Doing most of the real work, Asus eventually developed the capabilities to move into the consumer market on its own, using processes it had developed through blood, sweat, and tears.

To continue to make its return-on-asset goals, Dell outsourced more and more design problems to Asus, and at the same time outsourced its in-house capabilities for innovation and the responsive problem-solving process sometimes called "dark-horse prototyping":

1. need-find
2. conceive
3. build-test

As it stands now, Dell faces near obscurity. This would not have been hard to predict.

Companies that adopt agile practices cannot make the same mistakes caused by race-you-to-the-bottom outsourcing and other process-destroying tactics from the past 20 years.

SHIP
OF
THESEUS

Ship of Theseus

Christiansen compares Dell's outsourcing to the Greek myth of the Ship of Theseus, which was kept docked in a harbor for posterity as a tribute to Theseus' travels. However, as it weathered and aged in port, parts of the ship were replaced, until, eventually, all of the ship had been replaced.

The question is: Once every part of the ship has been replaced—where none of the original components remain—can it rightly be called Theseus' ship?

Is it not another ship entirely when none of the original components remain intact?

Although Christiansen's view of outsourcing may sound somewhat protectionist, it runs parallel to other sociological changes that outsourcing has created in American life, like hiring out all the house- and yardwork to downmarket suppliers.

That is to say, American kids don't take out the trash anymore. Instead, they are awash in excess resources like endless soccer practices, non-stop summer-camp schedules, and experience consumption.

The perspective is a bit home-spun, perhaps, but the point remains: We've outsourced a lot of our dirty tasks, but important capabilities emerge from doing those dirty tasks. Surely even Mom and Dad know: When you take out the trash yourself, it makes you think about ways to reduce the weight of the bin.

If agile comes from a roll-up-the-sleeves-and-let's-work mindset, you must have people on your innovation teams that know what it's like to roll up their sleeves and do some work, and that doesn't happen by paying someone else to do it.

Downward Mobility and the Innovator's Dilemma

Christiansen's more famous book is titled *The Innovator's Dilemma*, in which he put popular notions of "good" business management into proper perspective, saying real innovators have to throw most of that stuff out the window.

According to the creed, "good" management:

- Listens to customers and tries to serve their needs
- Cuts unnecessary costs with better efficiency
- Watches the market for what competitors are doing
- Invests more money in research and development

All of those things are what "good" management should do. It's what many business schools teach. It's an easy action item to leave conference rooms with.

But the big surprise is: disruptive technologies *don't originate from those practices at all.*

Christiansen says the old-school "manage better, work harder, minimize mistakes" approach does not create disruptive technology.

Instead, the creators of disruptive technologies:

- Do more with less.
- Test small ideas before trying them on a bigger scale.
- Adapt and change quickly.

Innovators don't usually need more money. In fact, they often need *less* money, because more money attracts more bystanders, more profit measures, and implementation of those "good" management practices, which derail real innovation.

Disruptive technologies have to be agile, and as such, in Christiansen's words, are necessarily "downwardly mobile."

Christiansen gives examples from disk drive manufacturing, to retail sales, to hydraulic excavators on construction sites: Disruptive behavior happens in every market, not just high technology and software. A disruptive technology is a downmarket entry that addresses future customer values, not the values currently attracting all the attention and business competition.

For example, in a market that demands faster and faster, a downmarket entry will be slower, but perhaps more durable. Durable will test its usefulness in many different ways, find a niche, and then—if necessary—get faster as a function of its durability.

That's how a downmarket entry eventually undercuts the market leader: He goes low and flips the script.

The Barriers to Downward Innovation
Downward mobility doesn't immediately glitter, especially not to Mom and Dad, who like the big numbers. Disruptive technologies are typically simpler, cheaper, more reliable, and more convenient. They may not be sexy at all, which is good, because the perceived weakness of disruptive technology is often its strength.

FLIPS THE SCRIPT

But a lack of overt sizzle isn't the only barrier to being downwardly mobile. There are other forces at work:

- The belief in upmarket profit margins through higher sales volume
- The tendency of existing customers in a market to want to move upmarket, too
- The inability of upmarket firms to cut costs, which get bigger and bigger (thanks in-part to expensive celebrity CEOs, who often cite upmarket movement as evidence of their value to a company)

All that upmarket movement is okay for sustaining technologies that are at the top of their game, like Dell 15 years ago. But disruptive technology is what will be at the top tomorrow, like Asus 15 years ago.

Going downmarket—or being downwardly mobile—requires quick adaptation, testing, and the responsiveness to find marketing opportunities in unknown lands. Innovation is not for everyone.

But consider this: Of all the books biographers listed on Steve Jobs' reading list, there was only one business book that "deeply influenced" him. It was *The Innovator's Dilemma*.

Euclid and The Royal Road

There's a story about being downwardly mobile—or perhaps about taking the hard road. As it goes, Euclid, the Greek mathematician, was brought to the king's court to teach mathematics to King Ptolemy.

The king listened to Euclid's lectures on geometry, but he couldn't understand them. He had Euclid explain over and over, but still Ptolemy failed to grasp it, until he eventually complained, There must be an easier way to learn this stuff!

To which Euclid famously replied, "There is no royal road to geometry."

There's no royal road to innovation or disruptive technology, either. If there is a road, it moves downmarket. The odds aren't good. The way is bumpy. The missteps are many. The hotels aren't as nice. The differentiation, imperative. The satisfaction, sublime.

The marketing that goes with downmarket innovation must be agile and downmarket, too. It must consist of small, testable ideas—not hierarchy-derived big ideas with big reveals and big strategies with big investment.

Agile is for problems money alone can not solve.

Emergent Strategies

That's not to say money isn't important. We all live in the real world, as far as business goes.

But if startup companies strive to be the most innovative, then it's worth noting most startups succeed only because they have enough money leftover after their original strategy and "big idea" fails.

According to Amar Bhide in his book *The Origin and Evolution of New Businesses*, 93% of all companies that ultimately become successful beyond the startup phase have had to abandon their original strategies.

Repeat: 93% of successful startups failed at their original strategies.

Agile management practices always strive to allow space and time for emergent strategies to develop, because that's where the real innovation opportunity exists, and that's the kind of opportunity traditional hierarchies crush with "bad money."

PLANTING SEEDS WHEN YOU NEED SHADE TREES

Good Money vs. Bad Money

The Theory of Good Money and Bad Money says, when the best strategy for success is not yet clear, "good money" investors should be patient for growth and impatient for profits.

That means, if you're being agile, don't blow huge piles of cash operating at a loss. Stay small and profitable on a small scale, until a growth opportunity finally emerges.

And since 93% of successful startups have to change strategies before they succeed, growing too big, too fast, without profitability is not the true path. Investors who demand growth before profits are the source of "bad money" in this theory.

However, once a profitable strategy emerges, startups must be agile enough to switch to a growth strategy—and be patient for profits while that growth occurs.

In the startup world then, abundant capital can fuel the wrong strategy, and it can fuel it aggressively.

For established companies, establishing a dual operating system is similar to having several agile startup companies operating within your hierarchy. Without agile processes, by the time you see the need for new businesses, it's probably too late to begin. It's like planting seeds when you need shade trees immediately.

You must invest long before you plan to see the payoffs. Put in your time before you put in all your cash. Water rows of seeds before you know exactly which trees will take root. That's the agile way.

Emergent Strategy and the Toyota Super Cub

In the 1970s and 80s, Toyota had a deliberate strategy to sell big motorcycles in America. They looked at the U.S. market and decided there was a good opportunity for more big hogs, like Harley Davidsons.

However, Toyota continually failed to break into the large road-bike segment. But that failure was Toyota's opportunity in disguise.

Their deliberate strategy failed, but an emergent strategy changed the game entirely. When money ran tight on the new venture, Toyota went small— really small.

Toyota made a wildly successful dirt bike called the Super Cub using money leftover after failing to introduce a large road bike to the U.S. market, where it was assumed only bigger would be better.

And they wound up selling more of the Super Cub small motorcycles than they ever envisioned. In the process, they also created a new market that didn't exist before—off-road motorcycles—where there was little competition and big opportunity.

Toyota marketing failed at first, lost most of its funding, went down-market, and reinvented the wheel.

FEATHERS DON'T CAUSE FLIGHT

Incentive vs. Motivation

Incentive is tricky. Incentive means, "Management gives you more money when you do the kind of work they want." But incentives will not necessarily produce the best return on investment in terms of innovation, happiness, or stakeholder value.

Consider: having feathers is *correlated* with being able to fly, but feathers do not *cause* flight. Lift causes flight.

Likewise, incentive is something management can create and is correlated with success. Big salaries, stock options, a new Cadillac, a set of steak knives, all that stuff. Strictly financial incentives worked in the Shareholder Value era, but in the agile era something more than financial incentive is required: motivation.

Creating motivation is not something management can do easily, but motivation is something much more valuable.

Agency Theory
In 1976 Michael Jensen and William Meckling published "Theory of the Firm: Managerial Behavior, Agency Costs and Ownership Structure," a study of incentives.

Jensen and Meckling's work helped ushered in the Shareholder Value Era by aligning the interests of executives (the "agency" of management) with company shareholders (the "principles" of management).

Agency theory has been dominant in business since the 1980s. Agency theory is what Mom and Dad lean on when they give you a few dollars for every A you get on your report card.

And that may produce straight A's. But straight A's may or may not mean actual learning is taking place.

"Straight A's can't hurt," you might say. It's correlated to learning. But it's not a cause of learning. All the straight A's in the world won't produce as many innovative problem solving skills as we'd like them to, any more than participation trophies win ball games.

Motivation Is More Than Agency

In his Two-Factor Theory, or "motivation theory," Frederick Herzberg says incentives are not the same as motivations.

Motivation means people do what they want to do in their work, where incentive means people do whatever management wants and pays them to do.

- Who gets stronger in face of failure? Motivated people.
- Who shies away from failure? Incentivized people.

Those are the two extremes in the Two-Factor Theory. Everyone would win if your company ran 100% on motivation, and everyone would lose—especially stakeholders, and eventually, shareholders—if 100% driven by incentive.

In practice, the workplace is a mixture of incentive and motivation. Creating incentives is one of the three measures of effective management, because 100% motivation is not possible. They are their own kind of complementary opposites.

Agile, with its roots in voluntary networks, prefers motivated people to incentivized people. This is why enthusiastic volunteers make better agile team members than those who feel they have to be there.

Satisfaction and a Lack of Dissatisfaction

Like motivation and incentive, satisfaction and dissatisfaction are separate measures.

- You can both love and hate something.
- You can be both satisfied and dissatisfied.
- You can be both motivated and incentivized.

Herzberg says dissatisfaction, or the lack of dissatisfaction, comes from increasing the levels of "hygiene factors" like:

- Compensation
- Status
- Job security
- Work conditions
- Policies
- Supervision

Herzberg says satisfaction, or the lack of satisfaction, comes from increasing the levels of "motivation factors" like:

- Challenges
- Recognition
- Responsibility
- Personal growth

Although hygiene factors can lead to a *lack* of dissatisfaction, hygiene factors can not produce satisfaction. Satisfaction comes from motivational factors, and having a lack of dissatisfaction is not the same thing as being satisfied.

The past 40 years of management history has created a business climate driven by shareholder value and external incentives via agency theory. In poorly managed businesses—which are rampant the world over—misaligned incentives and bad strategy suppress innovation as a byproduct of poor business culture.

To cope at these poorly managed firms, workers who would otherwise be self-motivated switch their thinking to a kind of short-term survival strategy, where they do whatever is incentivized while remaining open to new opportunities based on their real motivations—usually finding those opportunities outside their current firm.

Agile firms, on the other hand, seek to hire the kind of self-motivated workers who can thrive outside incentives. Agile—or at least the agile networks within a hierarchical firm—cannot exist without motivational factors, especially since many agile projects begin as small endeavors that might be dismissed as extra work from the mindset of incentive-driven action.

But that extra work is what those seeking satisfaction in their work thrive on. In fact, they require it.

As Harvard business professor Clayton Christiansen mentions in his book *How Will You Measure Your Life?*, it's when workers find work that satisfies both hygiene and motivational factors that they instinctively switch from short-term strategies to more deliberate strategies.

They switch from biding their time at a job where they are not dissatisfied, to charging after satisfaction at a workplace that fulfills both sets of needs.

When motivation and incentive come together, our rational Riders and our emotional Elephants can finally charge along the path.

iLook and Misplaced Incentives

iLook, a provider of ultrasound technology for natal clinics and hospitals, said their strategy was to sell small, inexpensive, handheld ultrasound equipment that was simple to use. By selling those models, they could act on a downmarket, emerging opportunity.

But iLook's compensation structure rewarded salesmen for selling bigger, expensive models of ultrasounds.

And while the company's salespeople had incentives to sell off-strategy tools, the company's engineers had motivations to make off-strategy tools: bigger, more powerful machines—not simpler, cheaper ones.

This misalignment between incentive and motivation is how companies with hierarchical management systems tend to flail in the face of opportunities:

- Sales follows incentives.
- Engineers make what they want to make.
- Marketers drink bourbon and cry at their desks.

But don't blame the salesmen and engineers. Both tend to be well-schooled at surviving in hierarchical systems.

The agile side of the dual-operating system must appeal to motivations and emergent opportunities in order for the business to thrive. Agile must say, "Hey, let's try a few cheaper ultrasounds, and see if it works."

iLook did.

Marginal vs. Full-Value Thinking

Christiansen says businesses tend to think their main constraint is resources, when in reality the constraint is a lack of process. Agile processes are designed to achieve difficult and rewarding innovations by priority—not by doling out resources on the margin—because agile is the process of full-value thinking, not marginal thinking.

Abundant resources tend to stymie innovation. At companies that have piles of cash flows to maintain, there's often no way (or, in the short term, no need) to innovate. They conform to the rule of marginal costs, a way of thinking widely taught in business schools and conventional economics classes involving making decisions based on the cost benefit analysis of making or selling "one more."

Marginal thinking is conservatism. As such, marginal strategies aim to protect business that already exists. The problem is: the business you protect will probably become useless or disappear, especially in competitive, quick-changing markets driven by technology.

The way an agile business thinks is not marginal. It is full-value. Agile asks, "If we had no existing business at all, how best would we build a new one?" That's not the same as, "How do we make one more?"

Many startups have no existing business, which seems like a problem, but it's really the biggest opportunity they have. Though producing on the margin may be cheaper and profitable in the short-term, it doesn't develop the new capabilities of process and priority, which is what startups should be doing at least as much as seeking resources.

For existing businesses, "leveraging" what they have in place to try to retrofit the business to a new opportunity is a tough task, especially if no process for such a change is in place and no culture suited to change.

That's how agile firms can do more with less. They go in small with the idea to invest more rather than apportion a minimum amount on the margin, quarter after quarter.

For example, routine paperwork is always cheaper to do manually for one more month than to absorb the full-value costs of migrating to an electronic system. That kind of thinking is how many firms continue with marginal-cost activities, year after year, decade after decade.

Christiansen says life—and business—is really a series of "just this once" contingencies, where doing something 100% of the time is easier than doing something only 98% of the time, due to the time and effort wasted in determining whether a situation falls into the 2%, "just-this-once" exclusionary category or not.

Agile always pursues new opportunities—100%—but makes small steps to test along the way. Change the entire paperwork system? Yes, but only after a small change has shown it's the right thing to do. Then act, always.

Leave discussion of "just-this-once" exclusions to the margins, where change is rarely anything more than a change in resources, budgets and plans.

The marginal 2% is where Mom and Dad do some of their best fighting, while the rest of us wonder why we still live above the garage in the grand scheme of things.

LIVING ABOVE THE GARAGE IN THE GRAND SCHEME OF THINGS

Marginal and Full-Value Thinking in Blockbuster vs. Netflix

As soon as innovation touched the movie rental business, the world of entertainment changed. Big, stable, wealthy companies like Blockbuster disappeared with tremendous speed.

Blockbuster executives did everything *right* according to traditional economics. They didn't go after the emerging streaming-content sector, because their marginal revenues in brick-and-mortar movie rentals were so high. So very high.

Blockbuster Video made 70% of its profit from late fees. Blockbuster made more money the more times customers returned DVDs late. It didn't matter how many times they watched it. Only that they returned it late. It was a cash machine.

Netflix, a company that charged no late fees with a DVD mailing business, made more money the *less* its customers watched DVDs. The less Netflix had to mail discs, the more customers their inventory of DVDs could serve.

So both companies had different strategies with DVDs. Why did Blockbuster fail and Netflix succeed?

When evaluating opportunity costs, conventional economics says ignore the sunk and fixed costs, which have already been incurred, and base decisions on the marginal costs and marginal revenues of the alternatives.

That's what Blockbuster did. Blockbuster looked at DVD mailing (and, later, online streaming) and said, the marginal revenue is too small for us to worry about compared to the money we make on in-store rentals and late fees.

If Blockbuster had not considered DVD mailing too marginal to worry about—had they gone in 100% and tested it—they probably would have been able to take much of Netflix's business before Netflix ever got off the ground.

Netflix, however, looked at the full-value potential of mailing and online streaming and said, We think this is where the world is headed!

Blockbuster feared cannibalizing its own brick-and-mortar business. They thought the business alternative to not pursuing Netflix was to continue along, making billions in late fees and not trying DVD mailing or streaming.

In reality, the alternative was bankruptcy.

CHAPTER FIVE

THE AGILE TOOLBOX

Most of agile requires the right mindset, but there are some skills that come in handy, like storytelling, hypothesis testing, giving and receiving feedback, and putting priority in the backlog for agile work.

Storytelling is Math

In 2004, researcher Daniela O'Neill of the University of Waterloo in Ontario gave children a story book with no words, *Frog Goes to Dinner* by Mercer Meyer. O'Neill asked the children to tell the story they saw in the picture book to a puppet who had never seen or heard it.

Some of the kids told a story about how Frog went to the restaurant and sat at the Table and grabbed a Fork and the Waiter came over and asked what he'd like for dinner.

Wonderful. That was the story alright.

O'Neill then asked each child to tell the *same* story again, from a different character's perspective.

Some children could do this, telling a story about Frog's dinner from the Waiter's perspective, or even from the Fork's perspective! These were the best storytellers in the group.

Those storytelling children later turned out to be the best mathematicians. Not the best writers. Not spellers. Not speakers. Not herpetologists. The best mathematicians.

Keith Devlin, author of *The Math Gene: How Mathematical*

Thinking Evolved And Why Numbers Are Like Gossip, explains this finding,

> "A mathematician is someone who approaches mathematics as a soap opera. The only difference is that the characters in mathematics are mathematical abstractions rather than abstractions from real-life people."

The link between storytelling and mathematics is vital for people who work in agile environments, because agile requires teams to see things from different perspectives and compile different user stories for different customers.

And they need to change those user stories as new mathematical data become available from their testing and measurement.

Storytelling has nothing to do with overall academic prowess, brain power, reading, spelling, verbal ability, or general knowledge. Storytelling also has nothing to do with calculation, computing, getting the "right answer" or following algorithms.

Storytelling is specifically linked to mathematics as a recognition of different perspectives and relationships.

The same way Frog and the The Waiter are entangled in a story, x and y are entangled in an equation.

Users who are "Slow Adopters" or "Digerati" are involved in a narrative with your business. As one thing happens to one character, it affects the other character.

SLOW ADOPTERS AND THE DIGERATI

An agile marketer or innovator learns to see these interactions at play for different customers, vendors and partners to their business, and he develops, learns and protects those stories as critical information to the business strategy.

Star Wars and Joseph Campbell's Hero Cycle

One thing about technology and software types: Everyone loves *Star Wars*.

Everyone knows the *Star Wars* story, and, at any given moment, is prepared to make a comparison, put R2-D2 in a Powerpoint deck, and do an impromptu Yoda impression.

Why?

Joseph Campbell, famous for his studies in comparative mythology, says *Star Wars* is a modern retelling of a hero narrative that's as old as humanity itself. In books like *The Hero With a Thousand Faces*, Campbell shows that all successful mythologies involve many of the same story elements:

- The Call to Adventure
- The Crossing of the First Threshold
- The Road of Trials
- The Transformation of the Hero
- The Master of Two Worlds

Lord of the Rings covers much of the same ground. As do many others. The point is that there's something about the software and technology industry that attracts those who like mythology.

That's a good thing! In fact, according to the research, story should not only be expected, but *elevated*, in places where mathematics are prevalent. It's the portal between the concrete and the abstract.

Telling stories is as old as humanity. It's how we relate to one another. It's older than mathematics. Or perhaps story and math are twin brothers in myth.

Campbell says our myth is ultimately what leads us to our bliss. He also says things are changing so fast in our world today that myth hasn't had the time to catch up. And the world has sped up since he said that.

For user stories to work best, they won't necessarily be tales about Aeneas hastening to the battle with his sword and shield. (Wasn't Aeneas *always* hastening?)

To create user stories an agile team can act on:

- You must be able to collaborate and create together.
- You must be able to read data and form and test hypotheses from it.
- You must be able to give and receive feedback in constructive ways.

Conventional Ideas of "The Right Stuff" for Business Success:

- Big resumes
- Steady running

- Resource-heavy
- Corporate structure
- Hierarchy rule

The New Ideas of "High Fliers" for Agile Business Success:

- Real-life experience
- Growth
- Process-heavy
- Start-up structure
- Network rule

Character and Plot

In their book *Rework*, Fried and Hansson suggest that, all other things being the same between two job candidates, you should choose to hire the better writer. Why?

Because of story.

For all our multimedia, words are still the seedlings of new ideas. Words help us to organize, express and vet. Writing things down makes sense of what we think—even before we know what we think. Writing is a way to figure out story.

Storytelling ability on your agile teams always pays off. As Fried and Hansson write,

> "That's because being a good writer is about more than writing. Clear writing is a sign of clear thinking. Great writers know how to communicate. They make things easy to understand. They can put themselves in someone else's shoes. They know what to omit. And those are qualities you want in any candidate."

As you collaborate on your marketing and innovation teams, always think, "Who are our customers, vendors, and partners— the characters in our story? In fact, what character are *we*?"

Working with agile teams, where the stakes are low and the dialogue more open than the hierarchy, helps train you to see the world from different perspectives. It's the same way Daniela O'Neill asked children to see the world. From the Frog's perspective. From the Waiter's. From the Fork's.

Try browsing customer segments from companies like Nielsen. That won't answer all your questions about your customers, but it will spark debates in your agile group and get you to start understanding different customers:

Are they "Young Digerati" or "Fast-Track Families"? Do they "order from Expedia and go water skiing" or "order from Buy.com and watch Country Music Television"?

The customer names themselves can elicit immediate characterization and images:

"Gray Power"
"Shotguns and Pickups"
"Beltway Boomers"

Fun stuff!

Plots

Joseph Campbell says our whole human narrative repeats itself. We repeat the same stories, whether in a cave in Sumer Valley or a cube in Silicon Valley.

And if we do have a mythology in the U.S. today, it surely runs through Hollywood and our cultural export in narrative: the movies.

As you think about the characters involved in your business, put them in context using the narrative plots that Hollywood uses over and over:

- Love—boy meets girl, loses girl, wins her back
- Success—the lead character has to win at all costs
- Cinderella—an ugly duckling is transformed into a beautiful swan
- Triangle—three characters in a romantic entanglement
- Return—an absent lover, father or spouse returns after wandering off for years
- Vengeance—a lead character seeks revenge
- Conversion—bad guy turns into a good guy
- Sacrifice—the lead character gives everything up for someone else's benefit
- Family—the relationship of characters in a single place or situation (e.g. hotel, office, prison)
- Forbidden liaison—social taboos, closeted relationships, adultery
- Jeopardy—a life-and-death situation calls on the survival instincts of lead characters

Think of the customer you're trying to reach as perhaps a "Young Digerati" character in a "Family" narrative. Give him a setting and a stride. Walk in his or her shoes to understand what happens to y and z in his world when x changes.

Authors Strunk and White criticize the businessperson's language in *The Elements of Style*. But they also touch on why business customers yearn to be cast in story:

> "The executive walks among ink erasers, caparisoned like a knight. We should tolerate him—every man of spirit wants to ride a white horse."

Agile marketers and innovators know fiction when they see it, and they use the strength of character and plot to their advantage.

Agile marketers are the curators of a company's story. They listen for the story. They track the story. They tell the story. They test to see if the story still matters. They put the story into new forms with new information. They keep the story safe when times get rough. They follow the story as it emerges and evolves.

- How someone finally seeks your services
- What a vendor goes through to manufacture part #45-334 for you
- What an investor hears in the quarterly speech
- What a four-year-old does when she picks up your product

User stories require expert telling and responsive listening. It helps to think of where customers are in the purchase cycle not as linear, but as a networked model where customers jump around.

Reaching a decision to buy is not a logical progression, but a blurred set of blended stages a customer can be in simultaneously at any time.

- Awareness—Do customers know they have a problem we can challenge them to act on?
- Comprehension—Do they understand we can help solve the problem?
- Interest—Do they care?
- Intention—Are they considering buying from us?
- Action—They bought from us. Would they recommend us or buy again?

Customers can go straight from awareness to action in an impulse buy. Customers can go from comprehension to action in a must-have purchase they have little interest or intention invested in. They can make a brand buy based on pure interest alone.

Buying is Emotional, Not Rational

Purchasing something is rooted in the brain, which does not function like a box factory conveyor belt. "Oniomania" is the compulsive desire to shop, and it's more related to mood-enhancement and identity-seeking than intention, awareness, or problem solving.

Even normal buying behavior creates an associated "buyer's high" and "buyer's remorse" in the mind, as summarized in the article "The Relation to Money as a Factor of the Consumer's Behavior," by Zorica Marković and Iva Antanasijević:

> "In the phase before purchasing, a prospective buyer often feels positive emotions associated with the purchase (desire, a sense of heightened possibilities, and an anticipation of the enjoyment that will accompany using the product, for example). Afterwards, having made the purchase, they are more fully able to experience the negative aspects: all the opportunity costs of the purchase and a reduction in purchasing power."

Emotion plays the same role in business purchases. Perhaps that's why "decision-makers" like their work and why problem/solution has always been the holy grail of B-2-B commerce:

> Because process devotees love to have an objective, rational justification for buying something that gives them a deep, subjective thrill.

An agile marketer and agile innovator knows this about his customers. Agile understands character.

MEET THEM
ON THEIR TURF

Hypothesis Testing, Data and the *n*th Degree

The interplay between creativity and data analysis is one of the most interesting aspects of the agile process. And it's one of agile's most promising signs.

Where Mom and Dad use analysis to fight over details, objections, mass-market targeting, and 2% exclusions, agile teams use hypothesis testing to get the minimum amount of information about what appears to work and what appears disproven.

And then they act on something learned from the tests.

There are no extra-credit points in agile for carrying out things to the sixth decimal place or taking things to the *n*th degree. Don't let Mom and Dad get you off the true path with their objections. "Character and plot? Harumph! We want tangible, results-optimized, market-driven, next-generation solutions...not storytelling!"

Funny how the serious prefer their own brand of fiction.

But the point remains. How can you go into the dark realms of linear thinking with agile storytelling under your arm and not get torn to shreds for your ideas? Hypothesis testing using solid data.

Here's a sad fact: Mom and Dad will not be prepared to meet you halfway on your agile turf, so you have to meet them on their turf.

Luckily, you know math and story are the same thing. And you don't need a lot of math. Don't get into a calculation exercise and debate. Do just enough to run a test and make a decision. If you know how to use this formula for hypothesis testing of two samples, you will already know more than a vast majority do about making decisions based on data:

$$z = \frac{(\bar{x}_1 - \bar{x}_2) - d_0}{\sqrt{\dfrac{\sigma_1^2}{n_1} + \dfrac{\sigma_2^2}{n_2}}}$$

This Z-test equation includes two samples of data, each with an average value (x_1 and x_2), a sample size (n_1 and n_2), a standard deviation which measures the spread of the data (σ_1 and σ_2), and the expected difference between the two averages (d_0).

All of it equals Z, which corresponds to a probability (which you can look up on a Z-table) that your hypothesis is FALSE.

A hypothesis, by definition, cannot be proven TRUE. It can only be disproven. Coming up with the proper statement of the hypothesis you want to test is difficult and a little tricky.

So before you test—for example, Ad #1 against Ad #2—you would NOT say,

"Hypothesis: Ad #1 *will be better* at getting sales than Ad #2."

Instead, you would say,

"Hypothesis: Ad #1 *will be no better* at getting sales than Ad #2."

Then you test and collect data to see if that hypothesis is in fact FALSE. If the hypothesis is FALSE, then that means there *is* a difference between the two ads.

How big is the difference? You can test for that by using a value for d in the equation. If you only want to know if a difference of any kind exists, you set $d = 0$.

How reliably can you say, "Ad #1 was better than Ad #2"?

That's what Z tells us.

Taylor Swift vs. Waterskiing Chimpanzees

Say we want to run a test to see which of two ads works better. We figure out our hypothesis and say,

> Hypothesis: An ad with Taylor Swift will not be better at getting conversions than an ad with waterskiing chimpanzees.

We go to creative, collaborate a bit, get two ads made, and place them both on five different media outlet websites over the same time period. Pretty soon, we have a pile of data about impressions, clicks and conversions (all of which are very small rates, so excuse the decimal points and don't worry about how small the measures are.)

WATERSKIING
CHIMPANZEES

We crunch the data to find the following:

> **x1** = 0.00045220, the average conversion rate for Taylor Swift
>
> **x2** = 0.00029387, the average conversion rate for Chimps
>
> **n1 = n2** = 5, for the five media outlets used for both ads
>
> **σ1** = 0.000348995, the standard deviation for the conversion rates for Taylor
>
> **σ2** = 0.000340377, the standard deviation for the conversion rates for Chimps
>
> **d** = 0, because we only want to test if there is a difference of any amount

We crunch all those values with a spreadsheet and get a **Z-value of 0.7262**.

That Z-value corresponds on a standard normal Z-table to a probability p-value of about .26, which means the probability that our hypothesis is false is (0.50 + 0.26) = .76

It's a way to quantify your guess!

We hypothesized that a Taylor Swift ad would be no better than waterskiing chimpanzees. What we found in the test is that we can say that's false and be right about 3 times out of 4—or with a .76 probability of being right.

Could still be wrong. There's a one in four chance of that. But if .76 probability is within our tolerance for risk, then Taylor Swift is what we should go with. Not the Chimps!

On the other hand, if we wanted to be certain to within a .95 probability that there's a difference between the two ads, then the averages and standard deviations and all the data would have to produce a Z-value of 1.645—considerably higher than 0.7262.

You can see that might happen if the x_2 value were lower, x_1 were higher, or the standard deviations were different. But even with a .95 probability, there's still a 5% chance that there's no difference at all in the two ads' conversion rates.

RICHEST PERSON
IN THE ROOM

Without hypothesis testing, agile experiments can get bogged down by the kinds of fights Mom and Dad have in the hierarchy—one opinion versus another opinion, with no way to measure between the two. Richest person in the room wins.

The Z-test is a quick and dirty way to add some certainty to your testing and data. However, as an agile marketer or innovator, you're probably not a statistics expert. The good news is, you don't have to be. There are plenty of software packages and people in your firm (or ready to be hired) who are experts.

Test whether A worked better than B. *What* worked—not *why* it worked.

"Why" is a rabbit hole. When you argue about "why," you will find yourself in the most inane discussions about whether the buttons should be blue or red and whether the call-to-action should be "Learn More" or "Find Out More."

Frankly, it doesn't matter. Why's will emerge with the more What's you figure out. Instead of debating, run a hypothesis test, and move on with action.

Test color. Test message. Test design. Test ketchup bottle locations on a shelf. Test everything. Test anything. That's what data is for. That's what agile is.

Like storytelling, hypothesis testing is more a matter of knowing what happens in the equation and what it can help you decide to do next.

The closer the Z-value is to zero, the more you can say the difference between two options is a flip of the coin—even if their average values are different. The closer the Z-value gets to 3, the more certain you can be that the difference between the average values is real.

Either way, don't spend too much time debating why a coin landed on tails.

Internal Feedback

In agile software development, developers can work and code in pairs—with one person typing like a driver and the other helping see the work like a navigator.

Those pairs are all part of a larger development team that holds short, daily meetings called "stand-ups," where members of the team share progress and prioritize what each work pair will do for the day. It's open and non-hierarchical in nature.

"Sprints" are the accumulation of several stand-ups and are focused on wider scopes, where bigger projects that arise during stand-ups are broken down into manageable parts, or "user stories." The team then tracks the progress of each user story on "burndown" charts. Burndown charts show what work remains on a user story or sprint, as graphed against time. Where stand-ups happen every day, sprints occur over a longer period time—one week, two weeks, a month.

What's the common element in all these agile components?

Communication—or, more specifically, positive feedback.

> Two people can't code together without constant feedback.
> Teams can't meet daily without giving feedback.
> Projects can't be broken into parts without feedback.
> Burndown charts can't be relevant without feedback.

But where a piece of coded software can be broken down into time-to-complete milestones and tested immediately to see if it works, a marketing or engineering idea takes more time to execute and try. Stories take time to develop. Progress can be harder to measure.

And unlike software, marketing and design initiatives involve more subjectivity and interpretation. Where there's subjectivity, there's the looming mistake of confusing correlation with causality. (For example, wearing an orange shirt does not cause your team to win, even though many people at the game may be wearing orange shirts.)

Because of the subjective shades of gray in agile marketing, giving and receiving good feedback becomes a critical element, or else the entire endeavor can quickly devolve into opinions, arguments, and hierarchy without proper testing and collaboration.

"You're an idiot."

That's one example of bad feedback. Though I'm exaggerating, sometimes criticisms of campaigns, design, headlines and other matters of subjective taste are as thinly veiled. Criticism of ideas for business direction or product improvement can get even more heated.

The agile marketer should crave positive, constructive criticism more than glowing praise.

Microsoft and Negative Internal Feedback

A practice called "stack ranking" created a negative feedback culture for years at Microsoft that stymied open, collaborative work.

Kurt Eichenwald took a pointed look at "Microsoft's Lost Decade" in *Vanity Fair*, chronicling how the company went from the most powerful player in technology in 2000 to a me-too follower by 2010. (The practice of stack ranking has since been discontinued.)

Microsoft's failure was an inability to be agile—to act on ideas that originated right under the company's nose: electronic readers, touch screens, social networking and, ultimately, operating systems.

The company instituted "stack ranking," where individuals are graded internally on a bell curve, meaning some people on the team always got an F no matter how well they performed, and others got especially bad feedback if they had "wasted" time coming up with frivolous ideas, like early prototypes for Facebook or touch-screen technology.

In interviews with many former Microsoft engineers and managers, Eichenwald says, "Microsoft failed repeatedly to jump on emerging technologies because of the company's fealty to Windows and Office."

Although the article places a heavy amount of blame on CEO Steve Balmer, Microsoft was probably filled from the top down with Mom and Dad managers that "knew" what would work. So certain that they couldn't be bothered to listen to seedling ideas that didn't fit their marginal thinking goals for Office and the keyboard interface.

Instead of working together on the new ideas with positive feedback, employees at Microsoft began to slit each other's throats with internal politics.

Instead of making up customer stories in brainstorming activities together, employees concentrated on stories about how to rank their coworkers—with self-promotion and self-preservation as their guiding light.

Positive feedback became impossible in that environment.

So how do you give positive feedback?
How can it help the agile process?

1. Describe

Begin any feedback by describing what you you *like* about an idea. If you don't see or hear anything you like, look harder. Find something—anything—positive. Without positive feedback in the beginning, there is no trust in collaboration.

2. Analyze

Try to interpret the meaning of what you see. What does the form or idea evoke in your mind? What does it make you think of? Now see it from the perspective of a customer and try to analyze how the idea fits into one of your user stories.

3. Evaluate

After you've described the idea and interpreted the meaning, you can begin to raise concerns or introduce why you think a particular execution may fall short of its goal. Try to make a judgement based on the criteria of the idea.

Criteria is everything.

Is this a huge branding and design campaign that will live on for a year or more? Or is it a web landing page with a shelf life of only a few days?

Temper feedback accordingly. After all, you wouldn't judge a child's self-portrait using the same criteria you'd apply to a Chuck Close portrait.

A

CHUCK CLOSE

PORTRAIT

In agile work, testing—not authority or criteria bias—settles disagreements. Don't judge the small ideas too harshly.

You don't have to have a rigid hypothesis in place before you test something, either. In his book *Ignorance: How It Drives Science*, neuroscientist Stuart Firestein says,

> "The trouble with a hypothesis is it's your own best idea about how something works. And, you know, we all like our ideas so we get invested in them in little ways and then we get invested in them in big ways, and pretty soon I think you wind up with a bias in the way you look at the data."

For whatever reason, traditional marketing departments have relied on hunches and authority when making decisions. Blame it on those Mad Men again. But for every Don Draper who's right, there are thousands who are wrong. And whether right or wrong, they all say the same thing, "Trust me, I know. This is right. That is wrong."

We'd all like to think we "know" what will work. But we don't, and those who claim to know can be catastrophically out-of-touch. Keep the feedback positive.

External Feedback

In *Market-Based Management*, marketing professor and former engineer Roger Best says your business's most profitable customers are the ones you already have.

Why? Because when you lose customers, you must replace them with new customers, and new customers are much less profitable than existing ones.

- New customers require more advertising dollars.
- New customers require more sales and service effort.
- New customers are furthest from "evangelists" than any other kind.

"Keeping good customers," Best says, "should be the first priority of market-based management. ...Customer satisfaction and retention drive customer revenue and the cost of doing business. Ultimately, they are key forces in shaping the profitability of a business."

Keeping existing customers is no small feat.

Studies show that, of 100 dissatisfied customers, only 4 will complain to a business.

Of the 4 dissatisfied customers who complain, 3 stay on as customers—a 75% retention rate.

Of the other 96 who *do not* complain, 91 exit as customers—a 95% exit rate.

But that doesn't mean those 91 exiting customers won't complain. As Best explains, "While market position is quietly eroded by exiting customers, attracting new customers is made more difficult because each dissatisfied customer will tell 8 to 10 other people of his or her dissatisfaction."

Best wrote these findings in 2004 based on data from 1986. This was before widespread customer use of Facebook and Twitter. This was before widespread use of online product reviews and ratings. This was before the social media revolution.

Dissatisfied customers—"terrorists" as Best called them and "trolls" as we might call them now—have only gotten more powerful.

If you have dissatisfied customers, they can now go online and tell the whole world. And they will.

Domino's and Negative External Feedback

The cascading effects of dissatisfied customers led Domino's Pizza to develop a program in the early 1990s to encourage their customers to complain. Domino's believed that if dissatisfied customers complained and the complaint was addressed quickly—even if not fully rectified—customer retention would increase.

By actively soliciting feedback, Domino's set a goal to *increase* complaint rates from dissatisfied customers. They also set a company goal to address all those new complaints within 24 hours.

The results:

Of 100 dissatisfied customers, Domino's increased the number who complained from 4 to 20.
Of the 20, they kept 15 as customers when they responded within 24 hours, and 2 when they responded after 24 hours.
That adds up to a 17% retention rate—far above the 3% retention rate Domino's had before it started the initiative.

Given the costs of gaining new customers, Domino's 500% improvement in retention rate of dissatisfied existing customers made a huge difference to their bottom-line revenue—all from changing how they encouraged and addressed negative feedback.

Social media has made platforms for customer complaints more available than at any other time in history.

Although every business is different, when you employ agile techniques to internal feedback, it will also show up in how you address external customer feedback. In a sense, you must first learn to respond to each other before you can respond to your customers.

Agile requires teams to develop a sense of class and decorum in how they communicate with one another.

Positive feedback isn't just feel-good, warm-and-fuzzy fluff. It's perhaps the most important lesson to learn from the agile process. If you take positive feedback seriously and make it part of your culture, customers will notice.

There's something dark in how digital communication frees us to say things in writing we would never say to people directly. Be better than that: Be positive.

The Backlog is Your Priority

In software development, the "backlog" is a list of programming work yet to be completed.

Management decides the backlog using information from daily stand-ups, feedback from the teams, and input from other stakeholders in the business who come together in the occasional meeting to decide what work—and, hopefully, what new opportunities—the business will pursue.

It's more than a to-do list. As in our personal lives, time is the most limited resource of all. Deciding what gets done first on your agile team's backlog is not a simple matter of list making.

The backlog says "These are our priorities," and it's a big deal.

Resources are *what* you have to work with.

- Skills
- Equipment
- People
- Cash
- Education
- Patents
- Technology
- Information
- Relationships
- Designs
- Brand
- Number of un-brewed pots of coffee in the break room cabinet

Processes are *how* you solve customer problems. This is how employees interact to turn resources into value. Agile is a process.

Priorities determine *why* you chose to solve some problems before others. Your values as a group of people, as a business, as an entity in society at large.

The backlog, then, is so much more than just a list of work. Implied within is the big question "Why?"

- Why are we here?
- Why are we doing this?
- Why do we have this opportunity?

"Why?" isn't something most people are comfortable with. So when the backlog is created, it cannot be left to the analytical side of the business alone. It's not a scheduling matter alone.

It's much bigger than that.

Agile processes connect marketing to innovation through stand-ups, sprints and a commitment to learn as you go along—a commitment to be fearless in the face of failure and never fail the same way twice.

The backlog connects the process to priorities, showing what you plan to achieve in an approachable and understandable set of steps. The backlog is the overall mission and is based on strategy, but it shows up in something deceptively simple and ever-changing: a to-do list

The big question is: Does your backlog represent the values you say you have as a business? For many companies, it does not. And for many people, it does not.

After all, it's easier to watch YouTube videos than to do the laundry. It's easier to do the laundry than clean out the garage. And it's easier to do all those things than to write a letter to an old friend, spend quality time with your children, or take stock of your progress toward bigger life goals.

Don't let the backlog devolve into a series of practical chores.

Agile processes should get the day-to-day things done while still preserving time to explore and question the overall assumptions those day-to-day things operate upon. Without priorities, what's the point of having an agile process? And without priorities or process, vast resources go to waste and disappear.

Culture is More Than Words

This book is not just about agile marketing and innovation.

Feuds like Mom and Dad's continue in big government, with plans, control and obsession with a promised future, and big businesses, with short-term goals, deregulation, and idealized past. These stalemates have been choking progress and innovation throughout the world, while polarizing wealth, opportunity and power into the hands of a few at either end of the fight.

It's a resource battle, heavy on wasteful processes, and dubious in its priorities.

Culture isn't something you agree upon in a meeting. Culture is something that emerges through a repeated process. It supports—or contradicts—what you say you are doing.

Culture doesn't come from a list of words like "truth" or "competition" or "freedom." It comes from the backlog of priorities and the repetition of a process for how to use resources to achieve them.

Actions speak louder than words. "Agile" is already a buzzword that's losing its meaning, like "green," "next-generation," "liberal," "conservative."

Rather than making a statement about culture, agile managers should strive to make statements of purpose.

Christiansen says, "Whether they want one or not, every company has a purpose—it rests in the priorities of the company and effectively shapes the rules by which managers and employees decide what is most important in each unique situation."

A Statement of Purpose has three main parts:

1. a likeness the company is trying to embody
2. a commitment to that likeness, and
3. metrics to measure the progress of fulfilling that likeness.

Clayton continues, "Companies that aspire to positive impact must never leave their purpose to chance. Worthy purposes rarely emerge inadvertently; the world is too full of mirage, paradox, and uncertainty to leave this to fate. Purpose must be deliberately conceived and chosen, and then pursued.

"When that is in place, however, then how the company gets there is typically emergent—as opportunities and challenges emerge and are pursued."

How you get there is culture.

Enron's Culture Without Purpose

Enron could be a case study for many things, considering how the energy company failed in an epic way in the mid 2000s.

Beyond the business specifics of Enron's deceit, the company gave only lip service to culture, without having a worthy purpose company employees could get behind.

At its height, Enron explicitly enumerated several points of culture, which included:

1. Respect
2. Integrity
3. Communication
4. Excellence

Blah, blah, blah. It all proved in time to be total b.s compared to the real actions common and encouraged in the daily processes of the company.

When it all surfaced, the company was done for, and people went to prison. Enron had a predatory culture—exactly the opposite of what it claimed— and one without a meaningful statement of purpose.

CHAPTER SIX

DRUMMER NEEDED

I've tried not to belabor the Mom and Dad metaphor. What I've hoped to do more than anything is provide a quick summary with case studies about why the current stalemate in our working world exists and what we can do about it:

> Shift our minds from resources to process and find new priorities in an agile era of information and insights, rather than ideological standoffs between blue and red, future and past, planning and gaming, regulation and deregulation.

Look at the two big hierarchies of Mom and Dad. Agile is only a child in that world. Luckily, it contains great promise and is growing up fast.

Whether implemented in a dual operating system or as the sole operating system, agile requires we work together on new ideas and take a challenger role to the problems ahead. To try something new.

Nature hates a vacuum. Without agile networks, the networks that form in businesses tend to have nothing to do with business, innovation, or providing better products and services at all.

It's not working anymore.

The solution isn't to allow everyone to work offsite or to farm it out to contractors. And it's not for everyone to go off on Daydream Friday and think of things with no deliverables and no actionable projects.

The Agile age—and specifically the dual operating system that will be its core—is a way to elevate problem solving, motivation, full-value thinking, emergent strategies, process and priorities to their rightful place: as complementary opposites to the ideological lines and over-abundant resources that dominate now, with long waits for big plans to be handed down from the fights at the top of the hierarchy.

Forget it.

The past 100 years have brought amazing gains in human society and cultural knowledge. Business has played a tremendous role in wealth creation and standards of living across the globe.

The Efficiency Era, Social Era, and Shareholder Value Era have all served their purpose to get us here, where scarcity is less a problem than over-abundance. What we do with our abundance is up to us. Mom and Dad could waste it all fighting.

Or we could start our own band.

It's time for new priorities in our work. It's time for new purposes rooted in motivational factors that produce an enduring culture, rather than the hygienic incentives that produce a world oddly low in both satisfaction and dissatisfaction.

It's time to move out of the house.

I have a friend who was a world-class downhill ski racer. She says every great athlete faces a moment during competition when they can choose to fail.

Sometimes it's just a little mistake. Cutting an edge a little too much into the slope. Leaning too far into a flag. Pointing a toe.

This flaw in performance she says comes from a fear of knowing that you might do your absolute best, and still not win. You give yourself an excuse.

Here's hoping for bravery every step of the way into the gates, to run again.

BIBLIOGRAPHY

"The Best-Kept Management Secret on The Planet: Agile," Steve Denning, Forbes.com, 4/9/2012.

"The Big Idea: Accelerate," John P. Kotter, *Harvard Business Review*, Nov 2012.

"Does Management Really Work?" Nicholas Bloom, *Harvard Business Review*, Nov 2012.

"Creating Breakthroughs at 3M," Eric von Hippel, Stefan, Thomke, and Mary Sonnack; *Harvard Business Review*, Sept–Oct 1999.

"Enron's Many Strands: Corporate Culture at Enron, Lavish Excess Often Came Before Success," New York Times, 2/26/2002.

How Will You Measure Your Life? Clayton Christiansen, HarperBusiness, 2012.

"I Consult, Therefore I Am," Steven J. Dubner, Freakonomics Radio, 11/26/2012.

Ignorance: How It Drives Science, Stuart Firestein, Oxford University Press, 2012.

Incomplete Nature: How Mind Emerged From Matter, Terrence Deacon, W. W. Norton & Company, 2011.

The Innovator's Dilemma, Clayton Christiansen, HarperBusiness, 2003.

Insanely Simple: The Obsession That Drives Apple's Success, Ken Segall, Portfolio/Penguin, 2013.

"The Management Century," Walter Kiechel III, *Harvard Business Review*, Nov 2012.

Market-Based Management, Roger Best, Prentice Hall, 2012.

The Math Gene: How Mathematical Thinking Evolved And Why Numbers Are Like Gossip, Keith Devlin, Basic Books, 2001.

"Microsoft's Downfall: Inside the Executive E-mails and Cannibalistic Culture That Felled a Tech Giant," Kurt Eichenwald, *Vanity Fair*, 7/3/2012.

"New Project? Don't Analyze—Act," Leonard A. Schlesinger, *Harvard Business Review OnPoint*, Mar 2012.

The Origin and Evolution of New Businesses, Amar V. Bhide, Oxford University Press, 2003.

"The Relation to Money as a Factor of the Consumer's Behavior," Zorica Marković and Iva Antanasijević, *Management*, (62) 2012.

Rework, Jason Fried and David Heinemeier Hansson, Crown Business, 2010.

Steve Jobs, Walter Issacson, Simon & Schuster, 2011.

Switch, Chip Heath and Dan Heath, Crown Business Publishers, 2010.

"Theory of the Firm: Managerial Behavior, Agency Costs and Ownership Structure," Michael C. Jensen & William H. Meckling, 1976.

Thinking Fast and Slow, Daniel Kahneman; Farrar, Straus and Giroux Publishing, 2011.

"U.S. Firms Hoarding $2 Trillion," John Aidan Byrne, *New York Post*, 8/6/2011.

"Where the Money Lives," Nicholas Shaxson, *Vanity Fair*, Aug 2012.

Jascha Kaykas-Wolff believes in two key principles: find opportunities where no one else is looking and never fail the same way twice—a methodology centered around Agile marketing practices. Coupled with a B.A. in Psychology from Whittier College, it's served him extremely well as an executive marketer and venture startup consultant at Yahoo!, Microsoft, Webtrends, Involver, Mindjet and, now, at BitTorrent. Jascha lives in Marin County with his wife Rebecca, three whip-smart children, four hamsters, two frogs and six or seven fish. You can find him online at *@kaykas*.

Kevin Fann believes great writing comes from both commercial constraint and artistic vision, that numbers tell stories, too, and that elegant ideas and shared human moments are the only stones worth mining. He has a B.S. in physics and a B.A. in English literature from Vanderbilt University. He lives where he ought between sea and cirque. *kfann.com*

Sean Martinez designs logos, packaging, music albums, t-shirts, posters, websites and just about anything else he can get his hands on, including collages made from grocery flyers and raw black ink. He believes simplicity is profound and that there's a lot more that can be known than can be proved. He has a B.F.A. from Pacific Northwest College of Art in Portland, Oregon, where he calls home. *seanmtnz.com*

Make people buy into CAPPM.

Made in the USA
San Bernardino, CA
31 July 2016